GRANDMOTHER EARTH II
1996

Other Grandmother Earth Publications:

Ashes to Oaks

Grandmother Earth's Healthy and Wise Cookbook

Grandmother Earth I

Kinship

Of Butterflies and Unicorns

Take Time to Laugh: It's the Music of the Soul

To Love a Whale

View from a Mississippi River Cotton Sack

From Life Press:

Bloom Where You Are Transplanted

Eve's Fruit

Mothers of Jesus

Our Golden Thread

Great Egret, *Casmerodius albus,* Barnegat Inlet, N. J.
Cover by Neal Hogenbirk
Waretown, New Jersey

GRANDMOTHER EARTH II
1996

FEATURING
AWARD WINNING
POETRY AND PROSE

Frances Brinkley Cowden
Marcelle Zarshenas
Editors

GRANDMOTHER EARTH CREATIONS
GERMANTOWN, TENNESSEE

ISBN 1-884289-14-2 11.95

FIRST EDITION: 1996

GRANDMOTHER EARTH CREATIONS
8463 Deerfield Lane
Germantown, Tennessee 38138

"We hopefully will stop to consider
All the blessings we've had since birth;
One of the greatest God has provided
Is our home--Grandmother Earth."

--Embree Bolton

Grandmother Earth Creations
was awarded
the second annual
Business Environmental Award
by the city of Germantown, TN
Environmental Commission
"for its pro-active role toward promoting
environmental awareness" by Sharon
Goldsworthy, Mayor of Germantown.

Grandmother Earth Creations prints all books on recycled paper in accordance with their philosophy of helping to preserve the earth. For the same reason most of the customary blank pages are omitted.

Black-winged Skimmer, one of New Jersey's endangered
birds; photograph by Neal Hogenbirk

INTRODUCTION

Our special thanks to Clovita Rice who selected the top poetry winners. This volume includes poetry and prose selected from among several hundred works sent by writers from across the United States for our second annual Grandmother Earth National Contest. We thank all of you who contributed and we hope that you will make it a annual tradition to send your best work for consideration. We plan to make it a tradition to find judges each year who will select poems that sing to each of us.

Although the contest allowed for the poems of any subject and any form, most of those entered expressed a love of and a concern for the natural beauty of this earth, its people and other treasures.

We are especially grateful to Patricia Smith and Dr. Malra Treece who helped with the editing and proofing of this collection. Without our patrons and volunteers, including Harold Baldwin and Barbara Abbott, Grandmother Earth could not continue. We hope that our readers will pick up the banner and make sure that copies of our prize-winning issues are available in libraries across the nation.

Frances Cowden
Editor

HOW IT IS AFTER

A telephone call and Monday went limp
and into shock and a dreadful
silence settled around and over us
like drifts of snow . . .

The calendar says Tuesday
and time continues
with blizzard gusts of wind
mouthing those ominous words . . .
There is no wrap to wear
against a death, but I borrow
your old brown down filled coat,
and finding a piece of peppermint
in your pocket, I hold
this small sweet burning memory
on my tongue and walk out
into a ruthless snowstorm

toward a Wednesday
and all subsequent days
 overcast
            with your absence . . .

                    Clovita Rice
                    From: *Slant*

FROM CLOVITA RICE

Thank you for asking me to judge the 1995 National Poetry Contest sponsored by Grandmother Earth. I enjoyed reading the poems. It is always good to know so many are writing and to find so many good poems.

And there were many, many good ones and it took many readings and re-readings to allow these top eight to come to the top, to prove themselves not only good but memorable and exceptionally crafted. The imagery in the top two will stay with me. Both writers made me feel that I was there sharing their experience and observations. They are poems I will want to read again, knowing there is still more to feel and see in other readings. They are ones I would readily accept for *Voices International*. What better criteria?

I do appreciate what you have done and are doing to encourage poets and promote poetry. Good wishes for your health and well-being and for the success of Grandmother Earth.

Clovita Rice
Editor, *Voices International*
President and Director
Arkansas Writers Conference

GRANDMOTHER EARTH 1995 NATIONAL POETRY CONTEST WINNERS

Judge: Clovita Rice,
Editor of Voices International

EDITORS' AWARDS:

SPECIAL MERIT AWARDS

PHOTO-JOURNALISM

PHOTOGRAPHY/COVER
Neal Hogenbirk, Waretown, NJ

PROSE

OTHER CONTRIBUTORS:
Only finalists who gave written permission were
considered for publications.

Celebrating Tennessee

Venustum album; a rare Paphiopedilum orchid from India
prized by collectors; photograph by Neal Hogenbirk

Photograph by Lois Batchelor Howard, San Diego, CA

NATURE'S PALETTE

Mountains
are
easels
of
old
nature's
palette
with
leaves
of red
yellow
orange
and
gold
floating
down
waving
in the
winds
like the
first
flight
of the
thrush
settling
to earth
covering
our sins
with
nature's
broad
brush.

Dallas D. Lassen
West Jefferson, NC

SESTINA FOR A WESTERN CANYON

Webbed in a phantasy of rock and pine
This mountain pass, aglow with layered light,
Prisms the miracle of timeless rhythms.
Cloistering creek and forest, bounding road
Are shale and sandstone walls in spectral shapes
That etch sharp peaks on sky. Rimming the valley

The running hills bend low. Into this valley
Each day slips, curving, settling blue on pine
And dun on cracked arroyo. Evening shapes
A slack noose of silence around light
That lingers. Shadows gather on the road
In ghostly congeries of glacial rhythms.

The mountains throb with wordlessness, while
        rhythms
Of storied years ride pompous down the valley
On winds that whine and clank along the road
Through heap and skid of dust. Dirge of pine
And ring of aspen voices merge and light
On water carving rock to garish shapes.

Under white half of moon, the eerie shapes
Of coyotes haunt the brush to deer's soft rhythms
On river stones. A badger caught in light,
Alert to moon-voiced cougar in the valley,
Quits stalking mice beneath a fallen pine
And moves to safer haven far from road.

2

Then mist, the morning's envoy, grays the road
And turns off stars. Soon dappled gold that shapes
And brightens slopes where sunflowers reach toward
      pine
Swells in the meadowlark's clear tonal rhythms.
Brief, brief the beauty shining in the valley.
Frail, frail these, these moments pearled with early
      light.

Millions of dawns like this have tumbled light
Over this canyon, old before a road
Bordered the stream. Torrents have racked the
      valley;
Floods, blizzards, summer droughts have altered
      shapes
Of hills. Pretending sameness, time's slow rhythms
Have carved on stone the saga, seed to pine.

Always shall light heap mottled shade of pine
On ridge and road as time, relentless, shapes
With wind and water rhythms, these walls, this
      valley.

Maxine Jennings
Ogden, UT

GREEN SHADOWS

The divers tell me where to search for shadows
And memories and swarms of spangled fish.
The valves are turned. Unheard, the solacing silence,
Like blood through arteries, and a singular peace
Descends. I feel the poetry of pebbles;
Air rushes through, a hollow, hissing sound:

Above my bubbles, bell buoy's siren-sound;
But, underneath these tides, toll only shadows
And glimmering, green-citrine light on pebbles.
With nets that neither hold nor free their fish,
The waters teach my porpoise heart their peace.
I hold my breath. The bell buoy bobs in silence;

It asks me if I come to worry silence
And why my land-world clangs with angry sound,
What need I have for more than green-flecked peace
Beneath this surface, to be caught in shadows.
The substance of my dreams is dreamlike fish
And mute sand where I drop gray thoughts like
        pebbles.

Remember when we flung our flat, gray pebbles
Across these inlet waters, broke their silence,
And stood as wordless as the words of fish,
When all we knew was love's self-centered sound,
Felt it surrounding us in green-silk shadows,
Gold sunlight that was womb-warm, full of peace?

How luminous of mind we were, at peace
With everything. We dove, and pretty pebbles
Of air went rising through insouciant shadows
As green as eyes of cats at midnight, silence
As elegant as eelgrass, and no sound
Disturbed the delicate, slow-finning fish.

How gentle are these curious little fish,
Come close to taste my fingers, stir the peace
Of limp liquid with tiny tails whose sound
Not even whispers. Nothing but pale pebbles
To gather; no harm, nothing but sweet silence
Of sponges; no hurt, nothing but green shadows.

And now, in silence, I become a fish
Who nudges pebbles, far from cluttered sound
Of cities, shadows circling me in peace ...

June Owens
Zephyrhills FL
From: *Poetry Society of Georgia 1993 Anthology*

NARRATIVE IN WHITE

The Innuit have more than ten words for snow,
nuances of texture, depth, duration.
My middle America snow is deep chalk dust,
prairie pages of the she-wind's diary.
She doodles idly, sometimes erasing her secrets,
terracing, pot-holing, dunning.

An old metaphor, the snow as an open scroll
for poets' musings. But this is not my tale.
A used quill lies on the river bank
where mallards write
their entries in precise graphics.
A raccoon's symmetrical syllables run bias
from pine margin to margin different versions
of blue and gray underscore each storyline.

I trace fox printing half a mile. The fox
hunts and pecks, rhythmically punctuating
with his nose. The theme, ancient
as the mouse, is polished, proofed,
sentimental quotations deleted.

The next page bears elongated strokes of a rabbit
accented by quick exclamation marks
of its cottontail. Over here -- a sudden cursive
shift, then wider spaces between its dashes.
I expect the paragraph to be followed by the fox.

But down here the plot changes. Hawk wings
interject a brief sweeping signature.
In an uneven indentation
the rabbit's sentence ends abruptly.

I retrace my rough scrawl
across January's broad shining sheets,
pondering how many small dramas my eyes missed.
And recalling the Innuit word for bloody snow.

Glenna Holloway
Naperville, IL

PRESENCE

The colossal ribbon
Of sky blue and white
Is tied luxuriously
About the round package
Gift-wrapped in
Mottled browns, blues, greens
And garland'd with flowers
Of every color
Ours through all time
To open
And open
And open
Still again

Lois Batchelor Howard
San Diego, CA

FAREWELL TO THE SNOW LEOPARD?

Atop a snowy mountain in the East--
Where winds of Asia whip the harsh terrain--
There dwells a much-endangered, feline
      beast,
In vigilant review of her domain.
The snowflakes fall and delicately land
Upon her grayish coat of spotted fur.
Her elegance is glorious and grand,
But destiny is overtaking her.

She senses only eerie solitude,
While nervously she flicks her bushy tail.
Extinction of her species could intrude
By draping her with time's eternal veil.
She's beautiful--this leopard in the snow...
That future worlds of man may never know.

Alan Frame
Youngstown, OH

SEATTLE WINTER

Swollen clouds hover darkly,
like a magician's massive cover
hiding tricksters in the earth;
maestro feeds the hidden crew rain, snow,
dark of long nights and pinch of days;
lightning flashes and thundering
       incantations
order legerdemain under way;
earth's microbes stir to their secret dance.

Huddled against the cold,
I cannot imagine what they conjure;
as always, I must wait the season
to know their spring display;
I've seen their show seventy-eight times
yet never guess its excellence;
memory reruns cannot equal the
       performance
but anticipation warms winter's chill,
baffles the cold and gloom
with musings of known yet unexpected
       wonders
that will make me laugh and applaud like a
       child.

Paul Barlin
Mercer Island, WA

MOTHER-FATHER

Poems closer than breath from my voice
trickle near your mouth, your cheek
Poems closer than my kiss slide like rain
off leaves into your hair so that your scalp drips
like earth's, shuddering and groaning,
changing heartrock to bonecave, to skull,
using wind, storm, pain, and death;
poems are love in the dark, poems are dawn
when they leap up and run into the white water
for icy swallows that quench and burn,
that strip your leaf skin bright against blue sky -
ashes to scatter at the end of one path,
to fight the beginning of another: see it climb!
It leaves this place like a crooked smile,
keeping its perfect match a secret
And look, the beaver and the she-bear!
Their motions also echo liquid cell and lightning
        strike.
We came of these, and like a breath, this is where,
with tangled hands and looks toward none, we now
        go in.

Linda Kay
Cabot, AR

TO THE ONE WHO FLY-FISHES WEST EACH SUMMER

(Upon hearing that poetic allusions to Yeats
are popular this year.)

The figure of a man
kneels by a stream
in Western summer,
waders immersed in Wyoming's Lamar.
Sunlight, like a light-weight shawl,
lies on his shoulders and head
round in concentration
over a trout, sized as two and a half hand spans.

The prize need not be proven to others,
save for four moose on the bank
and what the Minolta captures
before the delicate, underwater surgery begins:
gentle undoing of hook from lip
mild massaging of hands on scales
deliberate releasing of fish by man.
Both slowly disappear

into the widening gyre
unless the centre can hold.

Ellen E. Hyatt
Summerville, SC

11

BAPTISM WITH
WATER MOCCASIN

And the Lord said to Satan, "From where
do you come?" So Satan answered the
Lord and said, "From going to and fro
on the earth, and from walking back and
forth on it."
--The Book of *Job*

His bulk amazed us,
the way he'd maneuvered his folds
onto a switch of elm
directly above the baptizing hole.
After all, Cedar Creek offered
numerous spots for a snake
to wile away a Sunday, but only one
fit to baptize in.

Not even the brilliance
of proselytes, a rite of sheets
fluttering about them
in the early morning breeze,
had moved him. Not the most
floral, feathered, tasseled of hats,
nor the highest notes of a Doctor Watt
being held till the last thread
of their power--
nothing made him so much
as shift that bitter lozenge of a head,
shovel through the chilly fork of his tongue
to even feel us out.

12

It was as if he already knew
what was going on, as if
he'd been returning for ages
to blaspheme the Creek.

While the deacons
crawfished into place,
one could scan the bank of faces,
almost hear people calling up Scriptures,
favorite prophets to deliver us.
The sister in the blue crepe de Chine
sees Joseph released from Potiphar's prison,
and the old man there
with Stetson still on
is remembering Daniel in the lion's den.
Over there Jonah is being spat up . . .
Shadrach, Meshach and Abednego.
Everywhere shields were rising,
going forth against the tree.

A few boys with the story
of David and Goliath
burning their hearts
gathered stones to make war,
aimed to chuck the devil down
into the cloudy waters below,
but Pastor Gamble, an old hand
at this sort of thing, cautioned
"Leave him be, chillun.
Long as he up there,
we knows where he at."

Claude Wilkinson
Nesbit, MS
From: *Atlanta Review.*

LIVELY ORACLES

What is it then if stones speak
in soft code one to another, if
scarlet, gold and cinnamon leaves
scumble God's message on the hearts
of streams, if wellsprings spool

over their kingdoms of mink
and bream, revealing His aim?
What is it when a season's touch
pries a first violet from the scheme
of earth, when a certain air

means the last wink of blooms
should hide like drowsy animals
till the next green blaze--
what then when something that's not
the tongues of a thrush

or jack pines rushed with light
can open the body and change
the course of life? If just once,
there's a stirring that moves
on the blood, someplace where

we wonder who couldn't stay forever,
where we're made to think of swans,
to ask for their perfection, especially

their wings to lift ourselves
as white as the bones of a child.

Claude Wilkinson
Nesbit, MS
From: *Connecticut River Review.*

NIGHT OF THE BUFFALO

In the dark clouded sky
Buffaloes charge
Chasing stars they cannot see
At birth they were blinded
By the sound of the moon growing
Rain peels the fur from their hides
As the fur falls
It enters the earth
Then bursts into waves of shining grass
Here in America
The ghost of the Buffalo roams
Deer and antelope no longer play
They only browse on the grass
That is nurtured from the remains
of the forgotten

David Hernandez
Castro Valley, CA

ENDLESS MAGIC

The magic of the seasons
Touches nature routinely.
Bare winter, white and icy,
Sparkles silently.

A soft new green lights the trees
And springtime warmth melts the snow,
Birds exchanging mating songs
As rushing streams flow.

Summer skies awake hazy,
Turn bright blue with clouds of white;
Wildflowers color hillsides,
Insects chant at night.

When faded green turns scarlet
Trees and mountains seem ablaze,
And wind-blown dry leaves enter
That first magic phase.

Mary-Alice Wightman
Mechanicsville, VA.

From: *Thank You, Lord*
by Mary-Alice Wightman, (c) 1984

WASHDAY IN APPALACHIA

Washboard under her right arm,
sack of dirty clothes under her left,
my mother let me be
keeper of the homemade soap.
Hot feet pressed hard against wooded path,
couldn't wait to be submerged in cool wet.

The wide spot of the creek,
between greens of tall maple, became the washroom.
With back bent, she planted washboard legs deep
in creek bed where water rushed over hard rock.
Sweat beads rising on her sunburned forehead,
she scrubbed each piece of clothing twice.

Playing in downstream bubbles,
I could hear her singing
"What a Friend We Have In Jesus."
From the corner of my eye
I saw tears drop in soapsuds coming my way.
Suddenly, childish laughter ceased...

I ran into green woods, picked black-eyed Susan,
the color of her eyes,
surrounded them with baby's breath.
When I placed my offering
upon the alter of her heart,
she stood taller than I had ever seen her.

Janet Nesler
Sciotoville, OH

I LOOK OUT MY WINDOW

to see
if the world has gone away
and left my house and me
floating in empty space
Outside my window
scrawny geraniums
break contour of straw
where once a lawn grew green
the elm
drops yellow leaves
one tree stands wood-naked
fluttering leaves made shadow-pictures
but now twigs snap in wind
gaunt branches scratch
sides of a gray house
whose blinds are all pulled down
blackbirds on skinny legs
poke red beaks
into brown patches
and fly away into transparent skies
There are no people outside my window
they have all gone away to a green-shadow
place

Gabrielle Keller
San Francisco, CA

THE MOUNTAIN BLUE BIRD

A messenger of joy by color alone,
only early risers hear his
dawn song, like an echo of a song,
float across mountain meadows
and drift along forest edges.

He sails and swirls
and loops and lunges.
He plunges,
like a turquoise star falling
down a sun washed sky,
toward feasts of caddis flies,
grasshoppers, and gnats.

A herald of hope
in mind and myth,
an image of sanguine composure
even in gray moments of time,
the mountain blue bird swoops
through meadows of the mind
in undulating flights of faith.

James J. Isaacs
Dubois, WY

I KNEW AN APPLE TREE

I chose the apartment for the apple tree.
Out of my kitchen window
I knew the tree
With leaves fluttering, beckoning me.
I knew the tree
when it flushed with blossoms
for one passionate day,
zinging my head like a roller coaster.
I knew the tree
when summer richness dotted it
with cool-dipped apples,
young as childhood mornings.
I knew the tree
when apples dropped with days,
plunking like the basketball
dribbled by the boy next door.
I knew the tree
when the leaves warmed
like hundreds of dallying afternoons
that say "Come be with me."
I knew the tree
when winds blew and leaves sailed
and winds blew again,
until only a few leaves shimmered
like violinists' hands in vibrato.
I knew the tree
with bare, bony branches
and infinity of loneliness beyond,
but when two squirrels chased up the trunk,
along a branch, bending it low,
and arched to the next tree,
all outdoors knew Thanksgiving.

I knew the tree
when a setting sun
called out a glow from the branches,
and I knew that we were beginning again.

The next day the sound began.
Buzzing, raving, ranting,
raging, razzing, it broke the day.
At day's end I dared to look.
Humiliated stood the dwarfed trunk,
like a robot with stubby arms.
Nearby lay sliced limbs, neatly bundled,

their ends
glaring and naked,
and out by the alley
twigs of new life
stuck out of the garbage cans.
I knew an apple tree.

Dona Goldman
Highland, IN
From: *Dandelion Soul*

THE MEADOW
DOWN THE ROAD

There's a meadow down the road--
A gently rolling plain
With greenest grass, and
Snow white fence, and trees
Along the row.

There's a meadow down the road--
A peaceful island green,
Amidst the bustling building town,
Where cattle graze
And sleep beneath the trees.

There's a meadow down the road--
Thousands of acres still quiet
Midst man's turmoil.
It paints a picture
Of serenity.

Beware, yon meadow down the road--
They want your quiet slopes
And gentle hills
To grade into a flat brown space
For commerce. Soon

The quiet meadow down the road
Will be no more, and man
Will spread the earth with concrete
Steel and brick.

I weep in vain

For the meadow down the road.

Anne D. Babin
Collierville, TN

WINTER RIVER

Ice-crested wind waves splash
through an open channel framed
with jagged edges of iced shoreline.

Smooth stones, in shallow snow, poke
toward low sunlight for warmth
that will never seep into their core.

One lone gander, lost without his mate,
drifts ever widening circles
in a warm-spring pool and waits,
stung by winter frost -- alone for life.

James J. Isaacs
Dubois, WY

PHANTOMS PASSING

I went back to the old home place,
And wandered there awhile.
There were so many cherished spots,
And things that made me smile.
The wood gazebo there, I spied,
Half hidden in the trees.
I went and sat upon its steps,
And listened to the breeze.
It sang to me of yesterdays,
And picnics in the sun.
Of summer nights and sweet delights,
Of young lives just begun.
Where are they now, those children who
All shared this place with me?
And do they sometimes wander back,
If just in memory?
I stayed until the evening threw
Long shadows on the grass,
And all the stars in Heaven came,
To watch my phantoms pass.

Betty Lou Hebert
Coeur d'Alene, ID.

THE INTRUDER

You didn't even wipe your feet
    before you walked on my clean floor.
You brought primeval leaf-mold
    from the mystic forest, to leave
your loamy footprints on my tiles.

You brought the musky perfumes
    of youth and rapturous spring
to overpower the pungent odor
    of my pine-oil cleanser.
You allowed the wild, free wind,
    wafting wanderlust and pollen,
to come in the open door with you--
    to blow away my dull contentment
and leave living, golden dust
    on my newly polished tables.
You carried riotous, outrageous life
    into my ordered, barren house
to fluster and disturb my tidy soul.

Sheila Saunders
Juno Beach, FL

EVENSONG

The best time to climb the hill
that holds the deserted house
is late afternoon.
Poplar trees in the meadow cast long shadows
across the path's old score--
they creep like dark fingers searching for chords
along their roots' wandering base.
Sympathetic ivy hinges the door's last stand,
and fortune-hunting magpies meddle
with hopeful persistence
beneath the crumbling stucco walls,
their trumpeting cries muted
by overhanging eaves.

There comes a pause, fleeting as a sigh,
when color hangs heavy and gold
like the warmth of varnish on old prints
creating the last tone of day.
Smudges of evening pool the arriving stars;
then the sightless windows of the old house
lift their empty eyes
fringed with cobweb lashes
to where the sky renews its promise
that the coda played by sunset's soft hands
will restore their glow.

Joan Anson-Weber
Roswell, Georgia
From: *The Gate of the Year*

THE CALL

Once again the egret comes. It stands
on my window sill, balanced
impossibly. Still. Silent. Staring
in at me with the eyes of the marsh.

This has happened every evening since I came
to live in the city, where the moon
is only another headlight.

It doesn't stop there. All night long a flock
of crows peck at the marrow of my dreams.   Wrens
devour the stars like winter
seed, tear petals from the blossoming moon.

I'm afraid one night an owl may stoop
on me at the unprotected
edge of wake and sleep, may steal
me back to the rivers.
The cordgrass. The marshes. Forever.

Cappy Love Hanson
Santa Fe, NM 87501
From: *Breathing and Other Poems*, Plaid Falcon

MR. CLOUD MAKER

One day the sky broke open to searching eyes
saying there are no clouds.
No clouds cried the park children,
who will our string kite colors say hello to?
No clouds, cried the Colorado mountains,
our snow tops will have no one to kiss good
        morning.
No clouds, cried the weatherman,
my ten o'clock report will die to empty radar echoes.
No clouds, cried the gulf sea gull,
how can I hide from the tourists?
No clouds, cried young lovers,
how will we write goodbye love letters
when this day turns into low fog sadness?
No clouds, cried the sunset
how will I make days end a little brighter
without my orange and red lipstick
to put the west coast to sleep with?

They all ran to the hilltop,
only to find timber legs fast asleep in the dirt
        ground
and a bladed face
sitting silent to the wind's slow moving morning
        breath
and a water pump voice saying,
I'm sorry, I didn't think you would miss me.
I have been here so long and no one ever noticed
my sky art work that my wind brush blades created.
I didn't mean to disappoint the children

young and small,
or
adults strong and tall.

So if you find me broken down in summer romance
or frozen quiet in winter loneliness,
it's only because I don't talk too much
when my tin heart fingers get cut
by moving on breezes,
or when my "I love you's"
get lost in snowfall goodbyes.

I have made a cloud or two,
some eggshell white,
some love lost blue,
some sad war gray,
and
some thunderstorm black,
just to fit the moment.

So if
I should fall asleep again
be sure to wake me
with
a twist of the wind.

Tom Hendrix
Belton, TX

WOLF SONG

Listen to the lean wolf pack,
Howl a challenge to the night.
Silhouettes, stark on the hogback,
In the moon's surrealistic light.

Piercing the velvet gloomed silence,
With an eerie and ancient rune.
Filling the pine forest dense,
With a lonely, and ageless tune.

The lupines, damned by many,
But symbols of all that is free.
More hated and feared than any,
in man's lore, or history.

A creature, reviled and endangered,
Then nearly wiped out as a breed.
Destroyed by men that were angered,
Victims of avarice and greed.

Their numbers reduced by legions,
Surviving, as best they can.
Condemned to the desolate regions,
By the inhumanity of man.

Voicing their song of defiance,
With the innocent faith of a child.
Pledging eternal alliance,
By their primitive call of the wild.

May it resound along the Yellowstone,
And be echoed by Spirits past.

Hearken to the wolf song,
Home again, at last.

Earth Day '95

Christine Moyer
Lakewood, CO

CRICKET IN THE HOUSE

Weary from a day in field and kitchen,
grownups nod over the newspaper.
The lamp flickers in the breeze
that slithers through the screen door.
Sawing through the stillness,
a cricket taunts from a dark corner.
Mother springs into action, swatter in hand,
in search of the hapless creature.
She moves a chair, listens,
        moves the table, listens.
Ventriloquist-like, the chirping comes

from one corner, from another,
eludes the search,
From upstairs bed I listen,
secretly rooting for the cricket
whose cheery song
fills the dark with promises.

Now I, too, pursue a song in the dark
that veers away, away.
Just when it is almost within reach
its call mocks from another direction.
I stumble, curse, reverse my course again,
plunge headlong after the new source of the
        song.

Shall I, now the grownup,
with a fell swoop, silence
an already voiceless creature,
or keep forever moving old furniture
back into empty corners,
listening?   Listening.

Lucille Morgan Wilson
Des Moines, IA

DAWN IS A FRAGILE EGG
I BREAK WITH SINGING

I rise from pale wool of sleep,
shake numb fingers to life,
and fumble with buttons
on my saffron robe.
Passing the bathroom mirror,
I finger time lines around my eyes,
and go to the window.

The sky is the white of an egg.

Full notes of praise rise from my throat
calling lemon, gold, coral, painting the dawn.
Song and color lift together
luring from the shell of night,
the sun, a great golden yolk.

Awed, I turn wondering if it were I
or my mother who sang the splendor,
painted the sky.
Remembering other mornings,
I recall her stirring up a show,
throwing bright notes like silver sabres
from a highwire of sound.

It makes me glad to think
our songs are joined.

Margaret Cutchins
Auburn, AL

AUTUMN MORNING PRAISE

The late October morning is crisp and cool.
I shiver now and pull my thin windbreaker close
against the chilling wind.
Inside the weathered barn
the lumbering cows await their rationed
chunks of hay, apportioned from the stacks
of stair-stepped bales
that line the windowed loft.

In shadowed light
I climb the rough wood ladder
nailed against the wall,
to pitch down pungent provender
into the stalls below.
The fodder falls explosively,
and dusty clouds of musky sweetness rise
to permeate the warmed and sheltered air.

So, from my bird's-eye vantage point
I watch the hungry cattle chew
with calm, deliberate moves.
The rising sun now sends forth shafts of light
that pour through windows,
filter through the cracks.
Now tranquilized, I sense the peaceful hush;
and deep within, my heart reverberates
a soft Amen.

Dena R. Gorrell
Edmond, Oklahoma

Previously published in: *The Independent Review,*

Sunshine and Shadow (Gateway Press, Edmond, OK) *Living Streams: The Christian Writers' Journal,* and *Poet Magazine*

FORREST CITY - 1945

With the words, "We don't serve blacks in here,
go to the back door and I might give you one,"
I turn back to a time when I was eight, and two
children stood hungry for the cool taste of ice
cream on that hot summer day.
As the tears came and flowed down that small
black face, I heard a voice say, take mine.
Mother, seeing a child hurt by the indifference
of prejudice, handed the small boy her cone.
Her voice was kind, "Now you have one," she said.
I learned many things that day, but most of all
I learned that love is all colors-bright as the
yellow of sunshine and dark as the African night.

Betty Heidelberger
Sherwood, AR
From: *Lucidity*

THE SHACK

Broken glass
　　lies
　　　　in heaps
　　　and patches.

Dust blows over
　　sticks
　　　　stones
　　　　　　and whitened chicken bones.

Iron bolts
　　melt
　　　　into rusty puddles.

Falling nails,
　　rotting wood, and
　　　　tar-paper strips
　　sit
　　　　in piles, overgrown with weeds.

An old
abandoned
shack
shouts
the silent scream
of someone's broken
　　　　　　dream.

Betty Gysendorfer
Potts Camp, MS

RED FLAGS

They came closer today
marking my world with red
streamers on stakes,
and soon I will hear the saws
cuffing my trees
like a tornado slashing.

Machines will come
and ten million years
will be flattened, burned,
hauled away and replaced
by concrete, tamed grass,
and more people.

Then I will retreat deeper
into my woods and watch
as they make everything
identical.

Charles W. Cunning
Hot Springs, AR

SWINGING

The call echoed in waves
hitting my swinging body as I moved higher--
"Come in, time for chores,
water needs drawn, milk needs churned,
come on now, now, now--
back and forth, North and South
on the heavy straw-filled bag that
hung high from the old oak limb:
now, now, now,
reverberating in the hot August wind.

Boring chores were far from my mind.
I was hypnotized by the piercing blue of the heavens.
My thoughts were not of drawing water
but of drawing pictures
of what could lie beyond.

Soon before me a mirage appeared.
I saw new Kublai Khans,
new islands in the stream.
And with each passing vision of icy cavern
and robot elf,
a faint reverberating "now"
flowed quietly through my body.

The straw-filled pendulum slowed
as monotonous time drew me
into a pool of duty
where visions perish and eyes go up and down
in daily round

churning cyclic rituals
beating away the life of precious dreams
discovered on heavy bag swings.

John W. Crawford
Arkadelphia, AR

ORPHAN LEAVES

orphan leaves
like feathers

tremble

in a wayward
flow of air

coursing

on a fitful path,
guests of fickle wind

ADAMS
Burlingame, CA

MORNING GLORY:

A Butterfly

Delicately painted wings of steel
that stood up to abuse and torture.
Colorful neon dots
line the rutty wings.
Iridescent navy blue
shines in the sunlight
as she flies from my shoulder.
Her dainty legs softly crawl
up my arm; my love unfolds.
Her delicate feelers test my
gentle fingers that saved
her from the morning heat.
How softly she rests
by the morning glory flower!
How calmly she sits
on my wavering finger!
Someday I wish she would gather
her strength and lead me
to her butterfly friends.
But now, I laugh at myself
for thinking such thoughts.
For now, in a gold gilded frame,
her lifeless body is peacefully
resting; the blue on her wings
shining in the sunshine,
gleaming in my eyes.

Christina Meyer
Age 11
Silver Spring, MD

A DAUGHTER STARTS OUT

like a cutting.
A stemmy bud
clouding a place.
You go about your business.
One Sunday there's a pale reach
turns into tendril and root.
You go on vacation and when you get back
what you've got is this tough little vine
aching to grow.

A daughter, once she's here,
looks at you.
with this bright
knowing look that they say
doesn't mean anything.

Comes a night
you're so tired you're half nuts.
Half ready to half throttle somebody.
Two a.m. and she won't finish the bottle
she's too busy grabbing your thumb

and she stops screaming
yawns this wide goofy grin
lifts an eyebrow

and you hold her.
Look at her. Hanging on to your thumb.
When you can breathe
you laugh back at her,

catching on to what's going on, here,
how deep you're in.

D. R. M. Meeks
Houston, TX

MONSOON SEASON
For Robin at 15

A hurricane has whipped through you and landed in
your head
It's roared and howled, rattling around like so many
pennies in a jar,
screaming obscenities that make you forget

that you are not the storm
        not the hail pelting your heart
        not even the crisp shield of rain that drips
from your fingers
        and forms a circle of ice around you

A bitter wind has galloped through you and landed
in your heart
It's whistled and hooted, ransacking your lush
landscape

42

slamming your shutters, concealing all light, making
you forget

that you are not the dark
        not the ragged splinters lurking in comers
        not even the blustery shield of shrieking
squalls
        that cackles in the night, enchaining you

Sweetheart, exhale the song of wind and rain
that's been living in your bones
Step into the sun and breathe
Remember who you are, angel,
and discard the borrowed wardrobe of fear and loss
Accept your divinity, and
You are electric

Laura Cerenzio
Winter Springs, FL

MEMORIAL DAY

A sunrise rainbow arches above
snow-capped Oquirrhs like a benediction
after weeks of rain. I watch a gray
and white Seagull fly, carrying a stem
in its beak, think of Noah, sunless
forty days and nights in a smelly ark,
imagine his joy at return of the dove.

The last alfalfa field, unmarred
by hatchets of builders, pours emerald
mist toward green scent of willows
bordering canal where six yellow
ducklings paddle like a line of toy soldiers
behind wild mother. I think of Eden,
the pain of leaving.

I remember my father, holding fast
to his hundred acres of unpredictable
land, loving predawn solace of irrigation,
the cool quiet lapping around his boots,
untroubled by long-range goals.

And mother, sensing sunrise, shaking
out kinks and coals as she stirs fire
and rattles breakfast pots, fretting
into her endless mornings
that are no more.

The rainbow begins to fade
as did grandma's crepe paper flowers
crafted in lodge hours before Decoration Day
helping grass clippings bide
hard dry graveyard mounds.

Sun glints off carved mountainside
framing the Bingham Copper Pit
casting ongoing promise of gold
at rainbow's end.

Donna M. Oakeson
South Jordan, UT

WITH C0L0R BRUSH
FULL-L0ADED

Celebrating Logan Canyon
in late September

Van Gogh would love this canyon.
Vermilion in fringe of tangled vines,
these slopes riot with grand irreverence.
Maples in blush of late summer
flaunt their scarlet splendor
like sequined dance hall girls.
Aspens, gold in squint of sun,
clatter in sprung rhythms.

Color brush full-loaded, Van Gogh would capture
cloud bank and red bush glow;
rock face and slide of sun.
He would portray pines, pompous authority
as they bargain with wind for light and sky room.

In reckless colors and bold lines,
Van Gogh would define blush of leaf and stem,
rust of grass, and rush of crumpled bush
snapping at a squirrel's touch.
He would scrawl in ribbony scratches
hurry of seed pods in wind,
greenness of ozone-washed air.

Van Gogh would tell
how storm waits in convulsive sky,
its wrinkled ochre ribbons

45

streaming from clouds, nether sides.
He would paint in wide bands
of amethyst and blue
the certainty of change,
and the sadness that lurks
in speed of the sun's arc.
With lavish sweep of light and shade,
Van Gogh would show how brief,
how brief is beauty.

Brush fed by impassioned palette,
Van Gogh would save these prismed slopes
of gold and crimson, these skies
of pearl and pewter, this world
of ribald heights and shadows
for a wintry moment--

not as a magazine would picture prettiness,
nor as a movie would glamorize the picturesque,
but as a master. Van Gogh would paint truth,
rugged and glowing in summer verdure,
then glowering shrill as frost
in brown leaf clatter, eloquent
as the heart's nostalgic sorrow.

Maxine Jennings
Ogden, UT

MAN OF EARTH

I saw bibbed overalls, then saw the man
who leaned against an an ancient walnut tree
and, walking closer, I could tell their age
was timeless as brown eggs and butterflies
and beans. When this same man who tills the earth
can wait till Saturday to go to town

to buy Prince Albert in our little town,
and Daddy is the name I call this man,
somehow I knew we all belong to earth.
I knew it when I climbed that walnut tree
to question birds-and-bees, butterflies
and whys, when I was in ninth grade at age

thirteen. Perhaps thirteen became my age
of wisdom when I went to school in town
and only on my walks saw butterflies;
but always there was Mama and this man
each sturdier than any walnut tree
each everlasting as producing earth.

Although I loved the clinging feel of earth
within my hands from such an early age,
although I had respect for every tree
and every acre far away from town,
I had much more respect for this one man
who knew the ways of coons and butterflies.

And then one year I left the butterflies.
I left the solitude of soft black earth,
my brothers, sisters, Mama and this man,
to live in house-rows in a larger town

47

where no one neighbor cared my child-bride age
where no one even had one walnut tree.

Caught up in living, I forgot the tree,
forgot the golden wings of butterflies
and dug a niche within this concrete town,
until the call of black magnetic earth
pulled me back home. I stepped across an age
to see just once again an earth-held man

decaying like a tree. And then this man,
at one with butterflies and all who age,
passed through the town once more and joined
          the earth.

Verna Lee Hinegardner
Poet Laureate of Arkansas
Hot Springs, AR

GANYMEDE AMONG
BLOSSOMS

Moonless night has crawled away.
An apathetic sun rides low behind rock-strewn hills
and silhouetted pines.
I walk into fields beyond lodge-pole fences,
hear meadowlarks throat ten-note songs.

In the distance, a fifteen-foot pole protrudes
        from lupine,
Indian paintbrush, Queen Anne's lace.
An eagle perches there, controls me,
a fish, hooked and dangling, to be reeled in.
I stumble on stones, catch myself, slide slowly
        forward.

The sun goldens the bottom edge of clouds,
slips long shafts through oxeyes, and fireweed,
burnishes the trunk of a fallen pine,
haloes the stoic bird.

I crouch and inch toward it,
fall on hands and knees and crawl,
watching for slight movement,
recognition of my presence among fronds and
        blossoms.
The apparition holds my eyes, hypnotizes me
until I'm flat, slithering forward, barely breathing.

Without turn of head, or ruffling of feather.
the indifferent oracle lifts,

circles away on wide-spread wings,
makes an arc toward backlit pines, disappears.

Clarence P. Socwell
Ogden, UT

PAWPAW'S PLACE

The orchard trees are speckled red with fruits
And dropping over-ripes for honeybees.
Maturing corn is weaving tassel-shoots
Where purple peas are waves on verdant seas.
Behind a slatted fence with swinging gate,
A garden plot is rich in turnip greens,
Tomato plants are sagged with scarlet weight,
And climbing vines are puffing butterbeans.
When Pawpaw bought this farm, he was a boy,
Who worked it out by driving, logging, mules.
He much preferred his land to childish toy
And cleared the stumps away with borrowed tools.
Beside a creek where watermelon grows,
I almost hear him whistling down the rows.

Kitty Yeager
Arkadelphia, AR

AN INDIAN CHIEF SPEAKS

Remember, little ones, what you are told
About the shining water and the earth,
And know the heritage you should uphold.

Remember everything when you are old
About our ancient mother and her worth:
Remember, little ones, what you are told.

Man did not weave life's web; you can just hold
The strand you are, and have been since your birth,
And know the heritage you should uphold.

The rivers are our brothers, every fold
Of lovely land and every sparkling firth:
Remember, little ones, what you are told.

This precious kinship is your treasured gold--
So keep the flowering meadows as your hearth
And know the heritage you should uphold.

Love all beneath the sky which you behold,
Each living creature held within its girth.
Remember, little ones, what you are told
And know the heritage you should uphold.

Winifred Hamrick Farrar
Poet Laureate of Mississippi
Meridian, MS
From: *Mississippi Poetry Journal,* 1990

THE ORPHAN

The dandelion, like an orphan child,
Grew among hothouse flowers
Who haughtily lifted their heads and cried,
"She'll not last for many hours."

But the dandelion waved her golden head
And smiled at the world around ...
As her hours grew into days she spread
Strong roots throughout the ground.

The hothouse flowers smirked and sneered,
Tossing their silky heads ...
"The gardener will tend to this upstart," they
        jeered,
"When he comes to weed our beds."

But the gardener came and began to pluck
Not the orphan out of their way,
But every other flower from the bed,
Where dandelions bloom to this day.

Hedy Kolborg
Greenwich, CT

From: *Flights of Fancy and other Poems*
              by Hedy Kolborg

LEAVING DOOR COUNTY

The panorama of endless blues
  graces my right
And its serenity reaches into
my soul.

The verdant fields of full
  summer's bloom
Fill my heart and remind me life is good.

For this respite from our busy
lives
  I thank you
For all that stretches before me.

Like clusters of cherries on
these trees
  draped in God's design
These are made mine by the life we
share.

Shirley Rounds Schirz
Fennimore, WI

From: *Ashes to Oak*

GRANDMOTHER EARTH

1994 CHAPBOOK WINNER

53

GRANDMA'S ROSE GARDEN

Grandma is tending her rose garden
a smudged work apron
a straw hat that's molting
red scratches on arms
hands work-roughened.

She rests for a moment
leaning down to smell a rose;
she smiles to herself
takes a deep breath
and sighs.

Grandma snips several blooms
Pastel rosebuds of perfect form
to bring inside
to set in a vase
for placement beside her Bible.

She prepares a tea service for two
a cup for herself
to be filled
the other
not filled.

Grandma opens her worn Bible
reads the 23rd Psalm
then closes her eyes to rest;
to reminisce
with her soul at peace.

The rosebuds

beside Grandma's Bible
silently unfold.

Neal Hogenbirk
Waretown, NJ

CHICK-A-DEE--DEE-DEE.

Neal Hogenbirk.

During my final weeks in the office, before my retirement, I had daydreamed about nature adventures to come. I had already purchased the necessary guidebooks, from birds to wild-flowers.

It was the beginning of winter, just the right time to get a start on my daydreamed mall of backyard bird feeders. A heavy snowfall had delayed the creation of my mall. And so it was that I made a simple, flat feeding tray, securing it to the outside sill of a garden facing window. I then filled it with seeds.

The next morning I stood watch at my bird feeder window, while sipping on my second mug of freshly brewed coffee. In due course, the first customer arrived, a cute black-capped chickadee. The first thing that the perky little bird did was to hop right up to the window. It tapped upon it with its beak, and sang chick-a-dee--dee-dee just for me.

Only then did it select a sunflower seed and fly off to round up some more customers to make my day.

I could think of only one explanation for that unusual, but heartwarming experience, a chickadee's way of saying thank you.

After that, it was one chickadee after another, and tufted titmice too; each announcing its presence with a brief burst of song.

Later on, when my backyard bird feeder mall had grown, as I would refill each station from a pail filled with seeds, on many an occasion a lone chickadee would follow along. When I would set the pail down after a refill, it would hop upon the rim of the pail, and sing chick-a-dee--dee-dee-- and then select a nice sunflower seed.

Was this the same chickadee that gave thanks at my first bird feeder tray? Too far fetched, said my mind. But yes, said my heart!

Black-capped Chickadee; photograph by Neal Hogenbirk

FAMILY CIRCLE

Barbara A. Rouillard
West Springfield, MA

We would have to live underground for at least two weeks while we waited for the fallout to settle.

How would my mother ever clean up that mess? Would she get as upset as that time Mr. Kulik, the farmer next door, had his garden tilled and readied for the spring planting? For a moment, I thought she was going to cry. The grit from his raised dust settled like a mini-dust bowl on, and in, the ruffles of her Cape Cod curtains, and she had just spent the day before washing and spray-starching them all.

She'd probably have to make about a million trips to the barn to empty her *Electrolux* into the trash cans. Her dust rag would be wiping and snapping, *Pledging* away.

It would be expensive, an investment we, hopefully, (my parents always added hopefully) would never have to use.

Even the most basic model with just one room wasn't cheap. Never mind the deluxe (it was much nicer), with its many rooms to give parents privacy and to separate boy and girl children.

Beneath my parents' nightly conversations, as they weighed their options, I studied the glossy photograph of the catalog's cover.

The boy was stretched out on his cot, one of four lined-up like army barracks. There wasn't a wrinkle to the olive-green, woolen blanket beneath him as he skimmed his copy of *Boys' Life*.

The father sat reading a book on the edge of his cot, while the daughter stood by the mother, in their matching shirtwaist dresses. The mother was busy stirring the family's dinner over some kind of sterno stove with a thin, gold watch on her wrist still keeping time. There were many, many canned goods on the shelves lining the walls. Board games piled high, too.

It would have to be built in secret, absolutely no one could know.

A neighborhood's panic, even our relatives' fright, could cause us to perish. We'd have to scurry, with Dad locking, from the inside, the trap door above us ...

For a second, I saw Cynthia, the fat, Polish girl from across the street and the soles of her feet pounding on that entrance, where the bomb hit. For a second, I saw her skeleton flash through her skin like an X-ray, then her being instantaneously fried to a crisp. But...

We wouldn't see, hear, or feel a thing as we slept snugly, burrowed underground, like bunnies.

SCHOOL MARM VS MOTHER NATURE

Neal Hogenbirk.

When I was a young schoolboy I developed an insatiable thirst for knowledge. I loved doing my homework, and when it came to book learning, I was an eager beaver. I liked going to school; it was a release from the tedium of tenement-flat living. I sometimes wished that there was school every day of the week. That was what I wished during the long dreary days of winter, when nature was asleep.

When the first robins and bluebirds were to be seen, when the frogs at the pond touched off their strident mating chorus, my feelings changed. My thirst for knowledge by way of blackboard and books started to falter. Seated at my school desk on a lovely spring day, I'd listen to the birds singing, singing as though far away, as the trills and warbles filtered through the closed window. I yearned to be outside, my mind wandered, I began to daydream.

I'd forget where I was. I'd be down at the pond searching for tadpoles. I would see a huge bullfrog lift its head partly above the lacework of pepper grass, then stare at me inquiringly with its great bulbous eyes.

A rap on my knuckles, and the bullfrog dove out of sight in alarm. "Sorry ma'am. What was the question?" A few of the girls giggled and my face reddened. Later, after class, I pounded blackboard erasers, choking on the dust. Two more long months of school to endure before summer vacation.

I can't account for my my early love of nature, perhaps it was an inborn thing. I was only eight years old when I borrowed my first book on a nature subject from the library. It was a lovely book on selected wildflowers, with full-page sketches, along with descriptions and commentary.

I remember taking that lovely book with me on a Sunday picnic to a place called Mazda Park, in New Jersey--a park reserved for employees of the G. E. Company, of which Dad was one. We got there in Dad's "new" second-hand Model-T Ford, open touring sedan.

The park had a brook that kids could wade in, and a pool for the grownups. There was a deep covered well that required more than a dozen cranks to bring up the wooden bucket--a bucket that would be filled with ice-cold, crystal-clear water. Except for the mown grass surrounding the pool and picnic areas, all else was left to the designs of mother nature, meadows, woods and the banks of the brook. With help from my mom I was able to identify a number of the wildflowers there that were illustrated in the book. I think that this was as much fun for mom as it was for me.

The picnic at Mazda Park took place during the last week in May. A picnic that had intensified my urge to study the things of nature--a result of those numerous wildflowers that mom and I had identified. The final school month could prove to be a difficult one--school marm vs. mother nature.

On days when it rained, blackboard and text books received my full attention. No need for a rap on my knuckles on a rainy day. On days when the sun returned, I'd again become inattentive and day-dreamy, metamorphosing from a bookworm into a nature-loving butterfly. I wanted to be out-of-doors to let the sun warm my bare skin, as well as my insides.

I am now in my late seventies, but I am still as eager in my studies of the things of nature, as I was at the beginning. The study of nature is never ending, and I am glad.

Spring Peeper, *Hyla crucifer*, photograph by Neal Hogenbirk

INTO THE WOOD

Najwa Salam Brax
Flushing, NY

It was in Lebanon, my native land, on September first, just two days before my tenth birthday. The weather was pleasant and warm. While my parents were visiting my aunt, my eleven-year-old sister, Hala, and I decided to go for a walk into a wood behind our summer home. We wanted simply to hear the birds trill and to see winged and petaled creatures; we longed to observe animal life, to admire the native plants flourishing there, and to catch butterflies and golden scarabs.

Mom always worried about going into the wood. My sister's hobby was to collect butterfly wings, and mine was to catch golden scarabs.

As soon as we walked into the wood, my sister saw a vivid butterfly whose wings were adorned with rainbowy eyes. She quickly popped a small net over it, scooped it up and dropped it into her bag.

"Get rid of this bad hobby, Hala," I protested. "Butterflies are the most beautiful creatures."

Just as I saw a golden scarab, I tried to catch it.

"Hey, get rid of this bad hobby," my sister scolded me.

"I catch scarabs, I make them fly with my cord noose, but I don't kill them," I answered.

Then I enjoyed browsing through the beautiful scenery, singing to myself:

**With ethereal wings of freedom
wood creatures ecstatically fly,
Like bright-hued sparks of peace and love
spanning the undulating sky.**

Enthralled by the hustle and bustle in the heart of nature, I ran looking happily for golden scarabs. After a while, I looked around, but didn't see my sister.

"Hala, where are you?" the crisp air echoed the howls of dogs and the meows of cats along with my trembling voice. The wood was tossing weird ghastly scenes mercilessly.

The green grass was dotted with golden daisies, snow-white jasmine, ocean-blue iris, coral-red roses; and the ground seemed like a Persian carpet embroidered by skillful hands. Intoxicating perfume from the wildflowers wafted upon the air, blowing against my face, while the green grass and the overhanging trees were chattering. Nightingales haunted the air; robins assaulted the blossoming twigs and branches; creeping vines, like coiled snakes, stretched here and there; lizards ran around and turtles sunned. Spiders decorated the twigs with their webs; streams flowed slowly, whispering melodious music; joyful squirrels chased each other up the trees, then played on the trunk of an apple tree. I was enchanted by the exquisite beauty, its innocence and simplicity.

The more I advanced the more excited I got. The wood was beautifully dressed in a varicolored blanket, attracting both my eyes and feelings. Suddenly, I stared, unblinkingly, at a small body lying on the ground next to me. It was a dead butterfly. "Do I have the right to pick her iridescent wings? I thought to myself. "No, her wings still belong to her," I said in my silence. Then, I dug up the ground and buried her, singing this elegy:

> A few hours ago you were fluttering,
> how fast you fell down to the ground...
> tomorrow you'll flutter from twig to twig,
> and your rainbow-eyed wings will sound...
> Your death is but a short journey
> for a new life, soon you are bound.

I pondered over the death of animals; their natural home is their own graveyard. When injured, they have no physicians, no hospitals; when they are born, they teach themselves how to live and fight as if consciousness is born within them.

Tired and perplexed, I sat by a tranquil stream, gazing at the reflection of quivering bird wings in its ripples:

> Alone, I sit by a melodious creek
> listening to the mellifluous birdsong,
> I hear the affluent quietude speak,
> small and great creatures to one home
> belong.
> When the fresh breeze caresses every beak,
> wild visions twirl and swirl in every
> tongue.

The air was filled with confused cries of animals. Completely still, I waited for a spark of hope. My foggy thoughts raced though my mind. I heaved a deep sigh, then I began to move, inch by inch, never taking my eyes off the stream that entertained me.

Oh! A snake stretched its head up as if ready to squirt out its venom. I ran while arrows of fear assaulted my heart. Meanwhile, I heard growls from beyond a towering tree. It was time to fight, to defend myself. The branches of the tree were tangled as though they had declared war against each other:

> **I stared at the tips of the towering trees**
> **that challenged the sky and played with the**
> **breeze.**
> Haunting visions come to my mind:
> **and lovely dreams grow weird and wild...**

Looking around, afraid to walk, afraid to stop, I held my breath because I discerned the danger. The path grew dim and my feelings grew dimmer. I ventured into the wood, discovering lonely roads, coiled like snakes.

Trying to calm my heart, I looked at the sky. A cover of clouds was hanging over the wood, following me in loud undulation of laughter. A wind started to howl and roar through the towering trees. Suddenly, I heard a sneeze. I tip-toed in order to see my sister, I heard but my footsteps echoing in the stillness; my thoughts were thrown out by the howl of the wind.

I advanced carefully, then stopped, reluctantly, when I heard the squeaking of a rabbit chased by a fox. The poor animal was running desperately to save its life. I wished I could help, yet I needed someone to help me. Suddenly, I felt strength warming my veins and I bent to pick up a stone. I threw it at the fox. Luckily, I hit it and the rabbit was saved. Happiness and courage overflowed me; I really felt a strange thrill of courage:

**Where there is compassion and help,
there is neither danger nor yelp.**

Another sneeze caught my ears. Looking back, I saw shoes under a rosebush, I advanced carefully to catch mysister, "Hala, where have you been?"

Taken aback, I saw a young girl. "Who are you?" She asked me astonished.

"I'mmm... I'm lost. Oh, no, I'm looking for my sister." I told her smiling radiantly.

She rolled her eyes in a strange way. She was a good looking girl. Her blue eyes were as brilliant as crystal when she gazed at me. Her hair falling over her blushing cheeks was like golden sun rays. Her beautiful face was like a dewy rose. She was medium height, no older than twelve.

Soon after, I knew that Sonia followed secretly her parents and relatives to a charnel house where the body of her grandmother was lying. We zigzagged furtively toward that house and we suddenly met my sister.

All of us walked following the footprints of Sonia's parents. When Sonia reached her home, she said "Our meeting was by chance, but our friendship will last." She hugged both of us and a new friendship started. She was our nearest neighbor whose house was a half-mile distant.

Before we reached home, we thanked God for having arrived safely. We realized how fearful it is to be caught in a wood. I opened my small box and set the golden scarabs free, and my sister followed suit and freed her butterflies. We haven't hurt any small creatures ever since. Then I made this prayer:

Lord, thank you for giving us such beauty,
thank you for granting us a happy life,
teach me to be courageous and
compassionate,
keep peaceful my heart, keep patient my
        soul,
spare me from hurt, from fettering small
        creatures,
let me help weak beings into life's jungle,
stay by my side in dark days, in hard life,
your infinite grace fills both Earth and
        skies.

Monarch on aster blossoms; photograph by Neal Hogenbirk

67

Photograph by Francis Niven

CELEBRATING TENNESSEE

This section by Tennessee residents who were finalist in 1995 Grandmother Earth Awards honors the 1996 Tennessee Bicentennial Celebration. There will be concurrent awards for Tennessee residents in the coming year; winners will be featured in *Grandmother Earth III* along with national winners.

Photograph by Francis Niven

Photographs by Francis Niven

THEY COME

Francis Niven
Memphis, TN

Every afternoon they come, climbing the screen door, on top of the garbage cans, twined in the cast iron porch pillars. Looking through the window into the den, waiting, not very patiently for their daily handout, they squabble among themselves for the best places to see into the house. To see the man they love, watching for him to come to the door.

They come in all sizes from large senior citizens to weaning babies.

They come in four colors, normal, chocolate, shadow marked and albinos.

This dozen or so are just the first wave, the ones that live in the local trees. Later, visitors will arrive via their own superhighway, the storm sewer.

About fifty of them come every day for probably their one nutritious meal of the day.

When he opens the door, food bucket in hand, they tumble all over each other leading him to the feeding spot.

They've been coming for almost twenty years.

We welcome our little visitors. We glory in their beauty and grace. We laugh at their high-spirited antics. We thank them for letting us be a part of their family.

Our masked bandit friends. Our raccoons.

THE TENNESSEE

Along the river's edge
the golden lamp streams through broken
        clouds
curious as a searchlight.
Bridges, mountains and rocky cliffs
reflect, mirror-clear.
Down, deep down sinks the sky.
Splendid hues awaken the soul
and silent harmony repeats.

Margot Marler
Rossville, GA.
(Member, Poetry Society of Tennessee)
From *Tennessee Voices*

HAIKU

Standing tall at ease
colorful fall trees undress -
audacious striptease.

Jo Elliotte
Memphis, TN

PRAISE FOR TWO SEASONS

If I can stay another autumn
in this place, know again the fire
of sumac, hickory green and gold,
the oak trees' dignity in toning down
to brown while grasses hold
their summer, I shall require
no other joy, no other cheer,
for heartaches encountered coming here.

Winter here is wood colored, rarely snow
white, mountained leaves browning the ground,
stripped branches filigreeing dun sky, the glow
of fire logs, protective shading of chipmunk,
rabbit, squirrel. I, chameleon, blend
with lichened bark, plants resting to green
again, and wait here until winter's end
for earth's renewal of my dormant impulse to grow.

Florence Holmes Ryan
Memphis, TN
From: *Old Hickory Review*
       Tennessee Voices

CAPE COD MONOMOY WILDLIFE REFUGE

Your words still boxing my ears,
my eyes clouding over,
I fled down the path to the bay,
away from the car, that capsule of discontent
and away from you.

It was then I saw
their great white wings in the distance,
flickering on and off
in the tall marsh grass ---
milky slices of moon in the cloudy bowl
of the sky.
I stood and stared like a ravenous tramp
who has buried his tongue
and can barely taste
the simmering soup before him.
And yet like him I ate
in voracious gulps,
opening mouth and eyes and ears
and ever rose to that place
the hint of salt in the wind-cleared air,
the honeyed, grainy sand
so different from, our silky southern powder.

So foreign in every way, this quiet place,
like a new, exotic planet
even to us who grew up water-logged
from creek to lake to ocean.
Our Florida shores were sterile,

save for pelicans and gulls
and flocks of human kind.
Ours was alabaster sand, sprinkled with
broken shells --- beautiful dead things
colorful summer houses from which
all life had fled.
They were something like the ruins
of Pompeii. Those that were still intact
and large enough for show
had long ago been gathered,
deodorized, restored,
on view in shops for tourists.

But never this squirming plethora
of life, each rock alive
with barnacles and small brown horseshoe
crabs, wearing their fragile armor;
there too, small perfect starfish
lying warm and wet
and soft as new-born babes.

Even we in this nurturing place
found that our spiny surfaces were softened;
lay on the sand as warm and wet and calm
as any starfish newly spawned.

Pat Benjamin
Oak Ridge, TN

THE HAVEN

I have come to the pond.

At last it pulses before me ---
the center   the loving heart
    of the mother wood.
I have come. I have earned
my rest. I have somehow survived.

I sit in anesthetized pain,
only half hearing
the red-beaked gallinules cluck
and the wild croak of the grackles.
I am sitting so still
they swoop and strut by me,
surprising unreasoning fear   ---
a new thing in this place.

Will they fly straight into
my face, in their blue-black
darkness,   peck out my eyes,
taking them for a new exotic berry?

I move just barely, testing; they retreat.

The pond is gray today
unlike that day sun-dappled
 when I saw the gallinule ---
incredible in her green and
peacock blue --- bury vermilion
crown   in the fat green hyacinth
weeds, devouring purple petals,

one by one.

Today   a snake bird coils
his neck in black and gray
grotesqueries, from his fishing post
on a dead gray cypress stump.
He has been sitting there for hours
 with scarcely a nibble.

I can sit no longer.
I must walk ---
pace on the sheltered path
shrouded by twisted water oaks
and climbing vines,
where only the gaunt gray heron
hears me sob and I can immerse
this private death, in these waters
              crammed with life.

Lost in my confrontation,
I hush at last   mute
and immobile as the log I sit upon.
Nearby a small brown rabbit
nibbles leaves, and a diving coot
outlets his small white flag.

Pat Benjamin
Oak Ridge, TN

TROPHY

I

The old house echoes with emptiness
        and longing.
"Take what you want," my aunt said, but what
        I want
is Grandfather sitting in his chair, telling
a story, laughter in his eyes. Even the chair
is gone, siting idle in the spare room
at Aunt's house. Only odds and ends are left--
a dark painting, a tarnished lamp. I start
to turn away, empty-handed, when I see
Grandfather's prize trout above the fireplace.

II

"I was about your size when I caught that beauty,
knee-high to a grasshopper. I saved my money
from milking cows and picking blackberries
and bought the rod I'd been hankering for.
I snagged the fish right away, but he towed
my new rod to kingdom come. I hunted the
        creek bank
till I found it.   Lured by a dream, I risked
life and limb to best the beast of fish tale
and fable. Mid-winter, my feet froze in my boots
and I lost the end of my toe. Late Spring, flood
waters rushed down like the Red Sea when Moses
raised his rod. Swamped, I lay on the bank,
gasping like a fish out of water. I wore

78

the beauty out, pure and simple. One day,
when the sun speckled the creek like a trout's
            belly,
the rascal come out of the water with fins raised.
'I give up,' he said."
                    Grandfather laughed, enjoying
the story over and over, till he no longer
remembered it or recognized the trophy.

III

I take the fish from the wall and close the door.
I walk through the forest to the brook, still
sun-speckled, but troutless now, for only a school
of bitter brown acorns swims over the mossy
rocks. Clutching the trophy, I head for home,
a house echoing with emptiness and longing.

Elizabeth Howard
Crossville, TN

HAIKU

Below blackened peaks
Snow melts into bright cascades
Trout spiral in pools.

Thomas McDaniel
Memphis, TN

THE CAVE

We feared the cave
as lads are wont to do
but lured by parental disapproval
we stood outside
and felt the soft brown air
breathing in breathing out,
imagining beasts
of terrible proportions
that never lived in Mississippi.

Some, braver than the rest,
crawled up to the mouth
 and hollered out at monsters:
>   "Come on out big ole bear
>   or elephant
>   or whatever you are
>   You don't scare me none!"

Nothing came.
Nothing but the quiet
breathing in and breathing out
of the soft brown mouth.
We went to the cave
nearly every day,
 bulking up our courage
as young boys do:
>   "I dare you"
>   "Scairdy cat"
>   "You go first"

Some crawled in a yard or two

then scurried bravely back
to the warm summer light,
    "Naw, I ain't scairt.
    Ain't nothin' in there."
        "Why'd you come back out?"
        "Too dark to see nothing."

The Whaley brothers were the bravest
crawling in, feeling along
the walls and roots,
matches muttering in the breath
of earth's quiet mouth.

One day, in the rain,
seeking shelter,
the two of them crawled in.

Weakened by the rain
and time, angered perhaps
at being violated,
it fell.

We watched in ugly silence
as the grown-ups dug them out,
oh so still,
oh so muddy.

We learned of death that day.

William Holland
Memphis, TN
From: *Mississippi Poetry Journal*

ESCAPE ARTIST

Like honey splashed on black velvet
Your coat;
Your spirit free
not to be fenced in.
I thought you confined to
storeroom,
Then saw you crouched in grass
Stalking bird.
I thought you caged,
Then saw you on fence post
Grooming.
Sometimes you make me wonder --
Would Houdini return as cat?

Elizabeth Pell
Memphis, TN

IN AFFIRMATION OF NATURE'S WINGS

Lindberg said it first
birds/planes
"Let there be Birds"

after all feathers
are fallen

children of bird watchers
what's to see?

migration ballet
courtesy of video devices

children of bird-call lovers
what's to hear?

nightingale/whippoorwill
courtesy of audio recording

Ruth Peal Harrell
Memphis, TN

EARTHEN

They ran the sun in circles
Slowly like a dream and
Feathered water into clouds
To wet the earth beneath.

Coming home in sunlight
Coming home in rain
Gently chided for the love and
Being right again.

One morning it was over
So quickly rose the stars
That when the moonlight faded
There were paths upon the sand.

Edith Guy
Memphis, TN

HAIKU

On my narrow path
a shy cricket in my way
still . . . he was there first

Louise Stovall Hays
Memphis, TN

RUNNING WITH WOLVES

Spirit of the wolf
I am
In a woman's frame
Wise
And like the wolf
Impossible to tame
And yet there is
A way to share
The mystery
That's me
Let me show you beauty
In a moonbeam
In a star
In the hush of twilight
You'll realize who you are
Through the purple shades
of midnight
Our bodies disappear
Holding hands we feel and melt
Into what we hear
Our destinies are set
To be forever free
To look about the universe
And share eternity

Carole Fincher
Memphis, TN

INDIAN ATTACK

Small Panther drives his red Cadillac
round and round the trading store,
roaring obscenities, his long hair blowing
into his mouth, catching fire
from the bottle of whiskey, the shouted words.

Inside the store I watch Small Panther.
I feel his wild encirclement,
his words pound on my bone-stretched skin,
flash down my mind's valleys,
his arrows flame, his long gun roars.

Where is your horse, Small Panther? The horse
fire-leaping, strong-necked, black as the oil
underground, under your nails.
Where is the deer carried over these sands
impaled on your cunning, swift and sure,
slung on your fire for your woman to cook?

Small Panther drives his red Cadillac
round and round burning the dream,
shouting obscenities at the legend,
his long hair blowing in the circle of truth.

Rosemary Stephens
Memphis, TN
From: *Southern Poetry Review*

RAINLIGHT

Today's rain is bright,
it lights the grass
the pittosporum
the oak tree
with wet sun-fragments,
tiny pieces of broken
fire encased
in new-green drops.
Rain turns me
upon myself,
that watered beginning,
shuts out all
except the green
world and me.
The grass blazes,
the pittosporum bursts
into green flames,
the oak tree
drips green shafts
of light upon me,
starts in me new wonder
with new wet fire.

Rosemary Stephens
Memphis, TN
From: *South and West*

APRIL'S FATHER

The shrubs in front of his house
were planted in a precisely straight line
and sheared into smooth, round balls
each the exact size of the other.

He cut down the old magnolia tree
because it was always dropping leaves.
Magnolias do that.

He cut the big oaks in the back
because they shaded the vegetable garden
also planted in neat rows.

He kept on his desk a telephone,
note pad, and his name plate.
Nothing else was allowed
except for the folder he held in his hands.

His third child arrived inadvertently
because of his wife's forgetfulness
fifteen years after the second son.

His wife, illogically, he thought,
named her April.

She was different from the two sons,
who married quiet, dependable girls
and settled down to orderly desks.

April kept her room in disarray
and cluttered the house with her guitar,
watercolors, poems, and laughing friends.
Her father was profoundly disturbed

when April moved into an apartment
with her young man. He had meant
to walk down the aisle, accompanying April,
as a father is supposed and expected to do.

He didn't cut her out of his will
but he erased her name from the family Bible
so neatly and completely it was hard to tell
that April was ever there.

When April and her young man decided to marry
he was even more disturbed because he didn't
want to reverse the accepted order of things.

For the wedding in a park
April wore a short white dress
embroidered with red roses.
Her mother cried and embraced them all.

They dug his grave precisely
for they knew he would want it that way.

But April's noisy children
scattered red roses from the funeral wreaths
over the cold, wet earth
and in the springtime and all future springtimes
he was covered with rambling, tangled bushes
and masses of crimson, flamboyant blossoms
that dropped untidy petals.

Malra Treece
Memphis, TN
From: *Tennessee Voices*

89

GONE WITH THE
WHITE GLOVES

With the passing of white gloves
there went Southern womanhood
to say nothing of civilization.

In the lobby of the Peabody Hotel
where the Delta began
ladies wore short white gloves
or long white gloves
or medium-length white gloves,
or little bitty white gloves.

Now, no white gloves,
even with dress-for-success suits,
nor with designer jeans and boots,
not even with frilly summer dresses,

and there went the Delta.

Perhaps Vicksburg is still
in its original position.

During the gentle years
white gloves with a hat
to lunch downtown in a tearoom
and to buy new clothes to go shopping in.

White gloves, to ride to work on a streetcar.
White gloves, for Sunday morning church.
Long white gloves, while dancing at a ball.

(A ball is not the same as a line dancing.)

It was not the War Between the States
or Reconstruction
or the boll weevil
or Yankees moving South
or drive-ins replacing magnolia trees
that devastated the South.

It was the passing of white gloves.

Then, like dominoes, there went all the other
amenities.

I always meant to be a gracious Southern lady
but by the time I was old enough
and had enough money
a gracious Southern lady
had become an anachronism.

Malra Treece
Memphis, TN
From: *Tennessee Voices*

CUSTER'S MISTRESS

The Son of the Morning Star
Visited my village on the Washita
Before dawn on his Thanksgiving Day
Not knowing our chief was Black Kettle,
A friend to the white men.

To them we were all just Indians
And only good if dead.

Most of my family went
To the Happy Hunting Ground
That snowy morning.
Yellow Hair, breaker of treaties, spared me.

Although already with child,
He took me for his mistress.
"Me-o-tsi" was too hard for him to say
So I became "Monacita."
My body was his, but not my spirit.

For five years he kept me
Hidden from Libbie, but no secret
To the regiment. In time I bore him
His only son, Yellow Hawk.

He tired of me and I returned to my people,
Raised our child in the Red Man's ways,
And chanced to be near the Little Big Horn
When my ex-lover made his last stand.

For our son's sake
No tomahawk claimed Custer's scalp.
His goods were taken, but his body left alone,

Except that the squaws pierced his eardrums
So he would listen better
In the next life.

D. Beecher Smith, II
Memphis, TN
From: Zapizdat Anthology 1995 *Our Time is Limited*

THE DEER

Grace, beauty, swiftness
All in one
Like a feather
As light as can be
Trotting through the fields
Listening and smelling for prey
Like a bullet
Leaping and dashing from danger
Knowing every step he makes
The wonder of the deer trails
Like expressways in the woods
Not leaving a trace
Making its way from place to place

Daniel Booker
Age 13
Memphis, TN

CAMPFIRE SENSES

Yellow flickers paint
Faces in crescent around the campfire.
They dance in young eyes while
Hands hold lengths of striped maple
Topped with gooey white balls in
Varying shades of brown.
Some aflame.
Graham crackers and chocolate
Wait on the table beyond.
Laughter and conversation
Mask the eerie cries of loons
And the purr of forest
To all but me, smiling,
Standing, camera in hand,
At the fuzzy barrier between
Firelight and darkness,
Between sounds of campfire
And sounds of lake and forest,
Ready to preserve this moment
Among family and friends
And mountains.

Chuck Janack
Knoxville, TN

LAST SONG

The voices of the deep
one day may understand
why their calm sheltered waters
are devastated by man.

Poisons flowing freely
chemicals on every side
food supplies damaged
by oils and pesticides.

Twilight deepens into dusk
and the dance of the Dolphins end
playing tag with the Killer whale
who you desperately try to befriend.

The debts paid in full
after the slaughter is ceased
and Cetaceans sing
their last song of peace.

Angela Logsdon
Memphis, TN

NO RESPECT

"Man." (I refer to page three-eighty-four
Of Basic Freshman Anthropology)
"Is upon our planet earth
The predominate form of life."
This text I have expounded
To an arrogant yellow orb-weaver
Who crept from a porch chink
To web-twine my mailbox.
"Please note." I harangued.
"My opposable thumb.
My upright position, and my massive brain."
But the spider
Flouting superior cognition
And articulation
Continued to tat a doily
For my telephone bill.

Russell H. Strauss
Memphis, TN

CITY SYMPHONY

A quiet morning.
But not too quiet.
It is the city, after all.
A neighbor's air conditioner whirs and hums,
Taking a rest periodically,
As though it understood nature's life cycle.
Now and then a car lumbers by.
The train whistles in the distance;
An airplane zooms overhead.
Birds of various feather yodel and chirp,
Ranging with a myriad of barking dogs,
Hanging from bass to soprano.
Cats play, too, but they sneak about without a
          sound,
Their silence providing the studied rests found in all
          music.
The day is cloudy and cool.
My porch is a favorite haven
Where I sit and write my thoughts.
Presently the pitter-patter of soft raindrops
Sends the squirrels scurrying for shelter.
The drumming grows louder, and is soothing
          somehow,
Like a comforting lullaby sung by one who loves me.

Diane M. Clark
Memphis, TN
From: *Tennessee Voices*

RESPITE

There is just enough dampness
in the air at twilight
of the cool April evening
to lift the heady fragrance
of the honeysuckle vine
tenaciously twisting, twining tendrils
creeping into every bush
and crevice of the fence
its invasiveness boldly
attempts to choke all efforts
to keep it out of the flower garden

For a brief moment we forget
all desire to destroy
the source of the sweetness
as we stand in the dusk
and allow its perfume to carry us
back to the days before life's
dreams of romance were
in full bloom

The fragrance lingers.

Frances Darby
Memphis, TN

ACORNS

From my window I can see
Diligent bits of fur
Dart among the falling leaves
Hide acorns in a hurry--
Fast fill my faded garden
With their buried winter store.

September's scene brings home indeed,
The feel of Winter's night
As urgent need as well for me
To thrash my harvest crop--
And store within on my heart's shelf
Enduring acorns for myself.

Burnette Bolin Benedict
Knoxville, TN
From: *Kinship*

GRANDMOTHER EARTH CHAPBOOK
MERIT WINNER

REFLECTIONS

Wake of big barge
touches shore in a
rush, backs away, leaving
one unique piece of driftwood.

Cold rivulet trilling over
granite rocks, spray splashed by
elusive brown trout
glitters in the sun.

Dawn's oblique rays are
refracted by dew drops into
myriad tiny rainbows.

Early sunlight sparkles
from dew drops like
diamonds in the grass.

Cumulus clouds float
lazily across the sky
followed by a faint sound...
like harps being plucked.

Sullen, wrathful clouds
full of noise and fire; water evaporated
from ocean a thousand miles awary
creates gleaming pond in back yard.

Patricia W. Smith
Memphis, TN

GIFTS FROM
THE HERB GARDEN

Martha McNatt
Humboldt, TN

On my pantry shelf is a giant clear glass bottle, which my father found in the city dump many years ago. Each year I try to fill this and several other decorative bottles with herb vinegar. This year, it is filled with a beautiful rose colored basil vinegar. I also have a golden vinegar, flavored with thyme (and a drop of yellow food coloring), and clear vinegars in green and blue bottles. I enjoy sharing these vinegars with neighbors, and I often include a bottle in a holiday gift basket for friends or family.

Most herbalists, include the process for making flavored vinegars when writing about culinary herbs. I have recipes for vinegar flavored with everything from green walnut shells to pink rose petals.

Two methods are used for preparing herb vinegar. The method I use is cold pack which means packing fresh green herb leaves in a glass jar or bottle, covering with a good quality white vinegar and allowing to stand for several weeks.

A second method, which is quicker, uses the same procedure except the vinegar is heated. One disadvantage of this method is that some herb leaves tend to disintegrate from the heated liquid, and may result in a less clear product than the cold pack method, The obvious advantage is a quicker rendering of flavor and color, which may be an important factor for some vinegar makers, Flavor and color develop within a few days.

In spite of last summer's drought I managed to make several bottles of basil vinegar, using leaves from Opal Basil, which resulted in a beautiful product, the color of a rich rose' wine. I added a handful of sweet basil leaves to strengthen the flavor Opal basil is less intense in both flavor and aroma. Since the general rule for seasoning with basil is that it compliments the flavor of tomatoes, I plan to suggest the following recipe with my gifts of basil vinegar.

WINTER TOMATO COCKTAIL

Add one fourth cup of basil vinegar and one half teaspoon hot pepper sauce to two quarts of chilled tomato juice. Serve hot in mugs, garnished with a sprig of supermarket parsley. (Don't forget to nibble on the parsley for fresh breath).

My poor thyme bush was almost dry until mid-July, but I salvaged enough for a few bottles of thyme vinegar. The stems of thyme contain a large amount of yellow pigment, therefore the vinegar is a beautiful golden color. Thyme vinegar is my favorite for marinating chicken, which I cook in the oven with chunks of unpeeled Idaho potato. The recipe I will attach to my gifts of thyme vinegar is a variation of an old West Tennessee recipe for Chicken Doodle Soup, which my mother (who grew up in Bradford Tennessee where the delicacy is said to have originated) always served as an accompaniment to our Christmas turkey and dressing.

JESSIE'S DOODLE SOUP

To two cups of rich chicken or turkey broth, add chopped cooked giblets and chopped hard cooked eggs as desired. Season with three tablespoons thyme flavored vinegar, Add salt and pepper to taste. Serve over the corn bread dressing, Add water and reheat any left over to serve as a soup. More vinegar may be desired.

This year, I tried several mixtures of herbs for vinegar, but only one emerged as a favorite. The main ingredient is mint, which grows profusely in spite of hot dry conditions. The mixture included peppermint and marjoram, but the dominant herb is lemon balm, which is a member of the mint family. Uses for this vinegar center around fruit dishes. I make a hot fruit compote using canned fruits, which this vinegar will compliment, but the recipe attached to the gift bottle will be for a fruit salad dressing which I use as a topping for a fresh fruit plate.

MINT SALAD DRESSING

Prepare a package of lemon flavored instant pudding according to package directions. When the pudding has set, spoon out as much as you want for salad topping. Add an equal amount of non dairy whipped topping and mix well. Season with about one tablespoon mint vinegar per cup of salad dressing, Thin the dressing with more milk if desired.

One important factor in using vinegar for gifts is packaging. I found some pretty old bottles in my Dad's garage, but some of my gifts will be packaged in plain soft drink bottles with the paper labels removed. Holiday stickers, ribbons and one sprig of the dominant herb will add a nice touch to any gift bottle. Plastic screw top caps are good for packaging vinegar since a metal cap may discolor the liquid. I bought an assortment of corks to use with the old bottles. Decorating the bottles is, to me, an important part of the project, but the best part is that any amateur can do it.

HAIKU

Ice coated limbs trace
ghostly Spenserian script
across blackboard sky.

Harold Baldwin
Memphis, TN

CHRISTINE LUNDWALL: LITTER GITTER

Martha McNatt
Humboldt, TN

Christine Lundwall is a person who gets emotional about the world around her. Her environmental passion began on her daily walks along the streets near her home in Jackson, Tennessee. Her neat white house is a few blocks from North Highland Avenue, a once elegant neighborhood of historic homes, many of which are now rental property in various stages of disrepair.

Energetic person that she is, Lundwall began by picking up litter near the sidewalk and hauling it to her own garbage cans in a two-wheel garden cart. She soon expanded her litter gathering to vacant lots and lawns of unoccupied houses. Her efforts soon began to attract attention. Reaction to her project varied from "Woman, are you crazy? Let the city pick up the junk!" to one man who thought she had been ordered to do community service because of some offense. A few people stopped to express appreciation for her efforts.

As this spunky grandmother continued to pick up litter, a plan was taking shape in her head. She sought help from the Jackson City Beautiful Commission, to organize a litter-gathering campaign for Summer 1992, using school age volunteers to pick up litter on a regular schedule during the summer months. The City provided support services including tee shirts, but almost single handed, Lundwall recruited, organized and supervised the campaign.

By summer's end, North Highland Avenue had undergone a transformation, Lawn mowers appeared on lots long untouched. Occupants of apartments tidied up front lawns. The sight of young litter gatherers and their mentor inspired many city residents to become more litter conscious.

One highly visible building in the target area is occupied by a major Jackson law firm. The presence of large amounts of paper litter around the Dumpster raised the ire of Mrs. Lundwall. She picked up the litter herself, then marched into the building to request that more care be taken in disposing of paper generated by the firm. Her request produced more shock than concern, but the litter soon disappeared.

"Apparently somebody got the message," said Lundwall, with a grin.

Three years have passed since Christine Lundwall's Litter Gathering Campaign. She regularly pulls her garden cart through the neighborhood, but she no longer collects bags full of litter. A few soft drink cans, fast food wrappers, and plastic drinking straws collect along the area, but in general, the transformation which began in 1992, continues.

Christine Lundwall was honored with a Civic Pride Environmental Award by the Jackson City Commission in 1994. She has maintained contact with some of the students who helped her in the original campaign, and often is greeted by motorists who travel along North Highland on their way to work.

On a Saturday in May, 1995, Jackson City Beautiful conducted a city wide litter pick up day. City employees, girl scouts, and volunteers picked up almost five hundred bags of trash city wide. It was an emotional day for Christine Lundwall. Her pick up partner was Teresa, mother of Tim, one of the original student litter gatherers. Earlier this year, Tim's brother was murdered as he walked home from a friend's house. Teresa chose the area where her son was gunned down as the spot for collecting litter on that Saturday. Christine Lundwall ignored fears for her safety to accompany the grief stricken mother on her mission. "It made her feel better just to be there." said Christine.

The City of Jackson is better because Christine Lundwall lives here, but Lundwall insists that she has received the greatest personal benefit from the campaign.

Christine Lundwall --- Grandmother Earth salutes you!

HAIKU

Daring spider
empties herself of silk and
captures ladybug.

Barbara Abbott
Bartlett, TN

Nelle Weddington in her East Memphis wildflower garden;
photograph by Julia Hall, Walls, MS

AN INVITATION: COME SEE THE BORDER PINES

Nelle Weddington
Memphis, TN

If you ever have a problem similar to mine, a lot too large to properly care for, maybe you will want to experiment with my solution.

Never had I intended to buy a half-acre lot. I'd specifically told the real estate agent I wanted a small lot, "One I can mow." But somehow I'd gotten carried away with all the pluses of this one house: the old brick, the hip roof, the big den with a deep masonry fireplace, expansive windows and finally a row of pines along the back property line leading to the name I chose for the property, The Border Pines. The size of the lot escaped me until a visiting friend wrinkled his forehead a bit and said, "You've got a half-acre lot here. What will you do with it?"

My eyes widened. I gasped, "A half-acre? Really?"

Though my common sense cried out, Yard man, you'll have to have a yard man; there's mowing and edging, fertilizing and weeding, clipping and cleaning, my inner spirit was saying, Beautiful, wonderful, think what you can do with this place...

Soon thereafter the April/May issue of *National Wildlife* arrived and in it I found an article by Elizabeth Pennisi, titled "Planting the Seeds of a Nation." Outrageously beautiful full-page pictures of fields of wildflowers with intriguing captions grasped me. I hurried to read every word about wildflowers.

Right away I learned that wildflowers, often called weeds, are native to an area and will flourish at home. They require no fertilizers or water maintenance. Many are bright, showy and very hardy, reseeding themselves year after year, becoming a new way to landscape.

Because a plant in its native habitat is adapted to a normal water supply for that area, wildflower lawns could possibly have a big impact on conservation. What if lawns were flowing beds of lavender, rose and gold? If weekly mowing were only a memory? This was exactly what I was looking for.

The article warned me to be ready to wait a year or so before a lawn would be established. Some of the loveliest, longest-lasting perennials require more time.

Wildflower seeds are available through as many as 300 seed companies in this country, but gardeners should study the commercial mixes-- many will produce a one-year flash of color, then fade away.

A hard-working son-in-law helped with the initial labor of getting the beds ready and setting up the chicken wire for compost. Soon we were ready for the first seed and plants to go into the waiting soil.

Now, four years later, The Border Pines is a showplace. From March, when ajuga makes a purple mass down under the redbud tree, through the spring and summer, there come great beds of Sweet William, coreopsis, ox-eye daisy, black-eyed

Susan, Indian blanket, butterfly bush, chicory and a glorious spread of mist flower in October, attracting neighbors and visitors from over the city. This last fall goldenrod grew ten feet tall. The only problem has been the rabbits--they do like tender plants--but the table is full and I can always plant again.

There is no way to measure the rewards-the experience has been rich and productive with many opportunities to encourage others to plant wildflowers. Perhaps the best part of all is when I have time to sit under the maple in the late afternoon shade and slowly drink in the beauty which God provides. And I am thankful.

Photography by Nelle Weddington

OUR VANISHING WILDLIFE

Ouida Simmons
Memphis, TN

A Harvard biologist estimates that some species of animals are being eradicated so fast that at least five are consigned to fossildom each hour of the day. That is a rate of about fifty thousand each year.

The extinctions occurring now can be prevented with some sacrifice by humankind. To save the spotted owl, the eastern cougar and the ocelot would require the protection of their habitat. We humans would have to change our expectations of what our land can continue to give. The California condor, the bald eagle, the barn owl and other birds of prey, called raptors, are also endangered because their habitats are fast disappearing. They are encroached upon by human developers, their food is poisoned by pesticides and certain chemicals man uses can kill raptors outright. Some have thought raptors dangerous, but raptors feed mostly on mice, pigeons and other animals subject to overpopulation. All birds of prey are protected by both state and federal laws. Penalties can be fines up to $50,000 and/or one year imprisonment.

The river otter and many species of fish are also threatened. The straightening and widening of streams, called channelization, have destroyed habitats for them. Other threats to our streams include coal mine acid pollution, soil erosion, industrial pollution and impoundment of vital stream habitats.

Fresh water mussels serve as filters of water pollution and are good indicators of water quality. My home state of Tennessee has twenty federally endangered mussel species that face the same threats as fish. Several species of mussels support a multi-million dollar artificial pearl culture in Tennessee as well as providing shells to the manufacturers of pearl buttons.

All species of animals and plants, even one as seemingly insignificant as a mussel, are unique life forms that could possibly hold a cure for AIDS, cancer, muscular dystrophy or have some other manner of enriching our lives that we cannot predict. Some say extinctions are natural, but there is nothing natural about a species called man causing the extermination of other creatures by the thousands. Who knows how much longer *homo sapiens* will last if the destruction continues.

All news is not grim. The giant Canadian goose is an example of how an animal can be rescued from the verge of extinction, as is the rescue of the wood duck through the installation of millions of nest boxes. Bald eagles are making a comeback, hatching some young in 1983 for the first time in twenty-two years in Tennessee..

While we humans have been the culprits in causing wildlife to become endangered, we are also the key to their future survival. We are finally beginning to realize that whatever affects one part of an ecosystem or natural community affects all other parts, including us.

We can continue to work together to keep these magnificent creatures from quietly slipping away. It would be a travesty only to have them resurrected by the computers of movie makers after they are nothing more than fossils. We owe our children and grandchildren more than a celluloid illusion of the real thing.

Most of the destruction is done because of man's greed. Let's not forget a 19th Century Cree Indian saying,

"Only when the last tree has died
And the last river been poisoned
And the last fish caught
Will we realize that we cannot eat money."

ADAM and EVE

Myth or history?

Patricia W. Smith

Eve's Fruit
by Elaine Nunnally Davis

In her controversial second book (Life Press, 133 pages, $14.95), Ms. Davis clearly believes that the Adam and Eve story in Genesis is no myth or parable, but that they were real people who disobeyed God's instructions and were driven from Eden. She also puts a different spin on this disobedience - Eve was beguiled by the serpent because she "Was not enough like God, in her opinion, and she wanted to be more like God."

One of the more controversial aspects of this book is the role given to Eve. "Both Adam and Eve had sinned in eating the fruit, but Eve repented and accepted salvation. Adam did not."

"No negative connotation grew up around the name of Eve."

Much of the book is an explanation of these conclusions. Whether or not one agrees with Ms. Davis, after reading *Eve's Fruit* one will always look upon the creation story with a different perspective.

Down On The Ranch With The Crow's

Patricia W. Smith

Bloom Where You Are Transplanted
by Geraldine Ketchum Crow

In this engaging little book (Life Press, 134--pages, $11.95) Geraldine Crow tells of her adventures and misadventures as the wife of a struggling cattle rancher in the hills outside Little Rock, Arkansas. Mr. Crow had grown tired of his successful city career and longed to try his hand at ranching. With much apprehension his wife of many years went along with him.

Their first problem was that they were outsiders in a very close knit community. They tried to fit in, but seemed to always be rebuffed. After Mr. Crow had his first heart attack, however, the community as a whole came to their aid, sharing the husbandry chores Mrs. Crow was not able to perform.

There are many vignettes of their life, some happy, some sad, but always positive. They loved sharing this life with their grandchildren. Their only regret at leaving it after almost twenty years was that their grandchildren would miss the values and the lifestyle that only country living can impart.

Verna Lee Hinegardner
Poet Laureate of Arkansas,
announces her ninth book, *CHRISTMAS
MEDLEY.* This 64-page, perfect-bound book of Christmas
Holiday Poetry is $5.00 (Plus $ 1.25 shipping).
VERNA LEE HINEGARDNER
605 HIGDON, APT. 109
HOT SPRINGS, AR 71913
(501) 321-4226

In honor of
Eve Braden Hatchett
whose poetry continues to
Celebrate Life
in a beautiful and unique way !

A friend,
Lorraine Smith

In Memory of
Joan Marie Brandon
*who loved animals,
with love from friends
of her mother, Sibyl Grammer*

GREETINGS FROM
DR. AND MRS. DONALD H. EARL
GERMANTOWN, TN

118

119

FROM GRANDMOTHER EARTH
FOR SCHOOL LIBRARIES

Elementary and Middle School
Of Butterflies and Unicorns
by Frances Cowden and Eve
Hatchett: Focus on
Creative Writing; poems and
stories with environmental
theme through fantasy.
Perfect binding: ISBN 1-884289-04-5 $8.95; Library
Rate: $7.50

Middle School and High School

View from a Mississippi River Cotton Sack
by Frances Cowden:
Rural Life in Mississippi
County, Arkansas; family
values; love of the land and
the river; the magnetic pull
of the dreamer. Poetry /prose.
Cloth: ISBN 1-884289-03-7
$21.95; Library Rate: $16.

Grandmother Earth I: 1995
Environmental issues and
human values; award-winning poems and articles
by poets and writers from
across the nation. Perfect
binding: ISBN 1-884289-09-6
$14.95; Library Rate: $10
per annual issue.

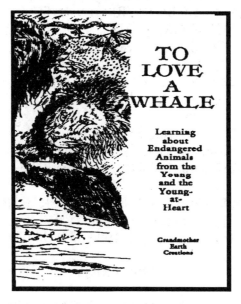

GRANDMOTHER EARTH

1-884289-01-0 VIEW FROM A MISSISSIPPI RIVER COTTON SACK--Frances Brinkley Cowden, paper, 1993, $9.95--1-884289- 03-7 ED 2--cloth, 1994, $19.95

1-884289-00-2 TAKE TIME TO LAUGH--Eve Braden Hatchett, paper, 1993, $6.95--

1-884289-04-5 BUTTERFLIES AND UNICORNS ED 4, Frances Brinkley Cowden and Eve Braden Hatchett, paper, 1994, $8.50

1-884289-O6-1 TO LOVE A WHALE--Frances Brinkley Cowden, Editor, paper, 1995, $11.95

1-884289-07-x ASHES TO OAK, Shirley Rounds Schirz, paper, 1995, $6.95

1-884289-08-8 KINSHIP, Burnette Bolin Benedict, paper, 1995, $7.95

1-884289-09-6 GRANDMOTHER EARTH I: 1995, $14.95-SUBSCRIPTION-- $10 per year

1-884289-14-2, VOL II, 1996, $11.95

LIFE PRESS

1-884289-05-3 MOTHERS OF JESUS, Elaine Nunnally Davis, paper, 1994, $15.95

1-884289-11-8 EVE'S FRUIT, Elaine Nunnally Davis, paper, 1995, $14.95

1-884289-10-x OUR GOLDEN THREAD Frances B. Cowden, Ed. cloth, $16.95.

1-884289-12-6 BLOOM WHERE YOU ARE TRANSPLANTED, Geraldine Ketchum Crow, paper, 1996, $11.95